A CHRISTMAS MUSICAL
FOR CHILDREN
ABOUT GOD'S PERFECT PLAN FOR US

CREATED BY
PETER AND
HANNEKE JACOBS

Lillenas PUBLISHING COMPANY
KANSAS CITY, MO 64141

CONTENTS

CHARACTERS

I Witness News Crew roles would be better played by older kids, 6th grade and above.

JACK: News Producer (can be played by an adult or a child) jaded and abrupt, always worried about ratings, dressed in a long-sleeved white shirt with rolled up sleeves, with a pencil behind his ear.

CECELIA: Reporter, very vain, should be dressed in a suit, always worried about her appearance and her comfort. She may use cue cards for any lines she delivers "on the air." She should have good diction and talk precisely. She has the lead vocal in "In A Palace."

TERI: Audio Woman, tomboy, dressed in work pants, T-shirt and work boots.

JOE: Camera Man, the "level-headed" one. He has been in the business for a long time. He is the only one who can handle Cecelia. Joe may be played by a person with a changed voice. He has a singing line in "In a Palace." Dressed in work pants, T-shirt and work boots.

ANNOUNCER: Expressive, clear voice, should have good diction, good microphone technique, and be able to project. Also able to time lines to the musical underscores. May be played by any age and is dressed in modern-day "business" attire. She/he may step in and out of the choir as necessary to deliver her/his lines.

BIBLE CHARACTERS

KING HEROD: May be played either by an adult or an older boy. King Herod has a complete solo on a vaudevillian "Herod's Song" which should be sung in character. His character is depicted as vain, self-centered and vengeful. Thus, he needs to be able to act angrily as well as vain.

SIMEON: A more serious, older-man character, he is the "teacher" in this story. Simeon has a complete ballad to sing with the choir: "Could This Be The Messiah?" We recommend this character to be played either by an adult or teenager.

LEVI: This servant of King Herod has the role of being the one who is the most affected by the birth of Jesus. Levi should be played by an older elementary-aged child.

WISE MEN: The three Wise Men all have short speaking lines and one singing line each. These parts should be played by the children.

SHEPHERDS: Although you can use as many shepherds as you would like, there are two shepherds with speaking lines. No solos are required of the shepherds. The shepherds should be played by children.

MARY and JOSEPH: These are not speaking parts, but rather should be played by children who can sit fairly still for long periods of time. The Baby Jesus should be a large doll wrapped in a baby sheet and carried by Mary.

Overture

In a Palace
Could This Be the Messiah?
Go, Tell It on the Mountain

Arranged by Peter Jacobs

SETTING: Center stage is the East Valley Mall. It is three days before Christmas. The I Witness News Crew (Cecelia, Joe and Teri) are getting ready for a live-remote broadcast. The choir is on the right side of the stage on risers. On the left side of the stage, Jack is pacing, a headset with a microphone on his head. A fax machine is visible on his desk directly behind him.

8

*"Could This Be the Messiah?"

10

*"Go, Tell It on the Mountain"

It's Almost Christmas Time

Words and Music by
PETER and HANNEKE JACOBS
Arranged by Peter Jacobs

12

14

CD: 6

Quicker ♩ = ca. 116

43 N.C. *Dialog begins

mp

(Several kids carrying bags with gifts walk hurriedly across the stage, some right to left, others left to right. The bags should be from the local mall, store or brand names to give a very commercial effect. Cecelia and the news crew are in position to conduct quick interviews.)

CECELIA: This is Cecelia Barnhurst reporting live from the East Valley Mall. There are only three shopping days left until Christmas, and…*(she stops a group of teen-age girls and addresses them on camera)*…Uh, excuse me. Ladies, who are you shopping for?

GIRL 1:   I'm getting a pair of earrings for my aunt.

GIRL 2:   I'm getting a pair of earrings for myself. *(she giggles)*

CECELIA: *(stopping an adult male)* Uh, and sir, who are you shopping for?

MAN: I've gotta find something for my wife or I'm in big trouble.

CECELIA: Right! And now, lets continue listening to this wonderful children's choir.

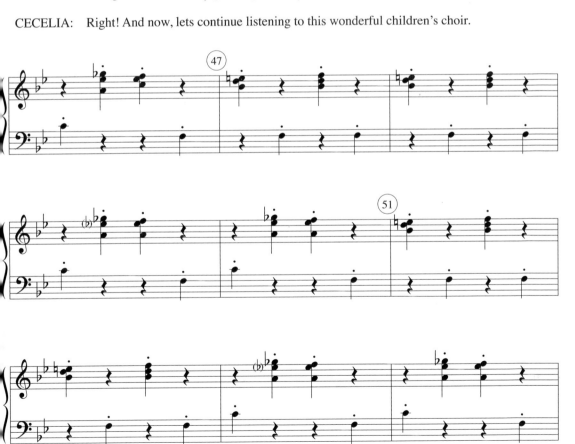

16

Cecelia: And Merry Christmas to all our viewers. This is Cecelia Barnhurst from your I
　　Witness News Team. Have a wonderful day.

News Trailer

PETER JACOBS

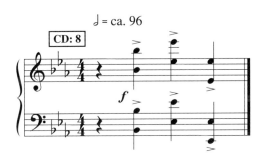

Teri: And we're clear!

Jack: *(into his mike)* Okay, good job, everybody.

(Schmultzy voiceover announcement at the mall interrupts him)

Voice Over: "Attention ladies! Today, for one day only, we have the lowest prices of the
　　season on women's shoes…now at your Village Shoe Store…"

Cecelia: A shoe sale? I gotta go!

Jack: *(taking the paper out of the fax machine)* Hold on a sec, Cece. Something big just
　　came in.

(News Crew walks across the stage to the newsroom)

Cecelia: Can't this wait, Jack? I HAVE to go to this shoe sale!

Jack: No, this can't wait, Cece! You guys have to jump right on this!

Cece: Honestly, Jack, you KNOW how I feel about doing these fluff pieces! And you just keep giving me more of them! I keep telling you, I want to do REAL news!

Joe: When have you ever objected to going to the mall, huh, Cece? Come on! You practically LIVE there anyway!

Cece: *(deliberately)* Shopping is entirely different from doing a remote, Joe! And besides *(she fluffs her hair)* now that I'm a celebrity, people just keep stopping me!

Jack: Well, then I guess a shoe sale should be out of the question!

Cecelia: Argh!!! *(exasperated, she throws her hands up in the air)*

Jack: There's no time to argue about this. The network wants us to break this story, NOW. Here's the report, Cece.

(Jack hands the fax to Cece)

Teri: All right. Stand by everyone.

I Witness News Theme

PETER JACOBS

*Announcer: We interrupt this program to bring you a breaking news story. Here now, is our
I Witness News correspondent, Cecelia Barnhurst. Cecelia?

Cecelia: An unidentified celestial object has been spotted in the Middle East, moving steadily
across the sky, traveling in a westward direction. Scientists say that, based on the
UFO's trajectory, it appears to be headed somewhere just south of Jerusalem, possibly
near the small town of Bethlehem.

In what could be a related story, the Israeli citizens are reportedly traveling in record
numbers. Reports just now coming in say that everyone has been ordered back to the
place of their birth by Emperor Caesar Augustus. Traffic is tied up in every direction,
and every hotel is booked up solid throughout the region. We'll have updates for you
as they become available. This is Cecelia Barnhurst for I Witness News.

Teri: And we're clear.

Jack: Now you three go pack your bags. I'm sending you over there right now to investigate
this story! You can use the time-delay satellite to make your reports.

Cecelia: Excuuuuse me! I can't go to Israel NOW, Jack!

Jack: *(sarcastically)* And why not? You need to be at a shoe sale?

Cecelia: It's Christmas, Jack! I have plans!

Jack: Didn't I just hear you complain about fluff pieces again? Do you want to do a real story
here, or…maybe you'd rather go back to doing the weather?

Cecelia: But Jack! I'm supposed to go skiing! I just got a whole new outfit.

Jack: This is not a request, Cece. Okay, it says here you will be arriving at King Herod's
palace in Jerusalem, just in time to interview three Wise Men from the East, who have
been tracking this UFO. Start with them and see where the story leads you.

Cecelia: Unbelievable! You're sending me to the middle of the desert at Christmastime,
expecting me to drop all my plans, and go to…*(suddenly her whole tone changes)*
Wait a minute. Did you say a PALACE?!!

Jack: That's right. King Herod's Palace.

Cecelia: *(suddenly making up her mind)* All right. I'll do it…for the network.

Jack: Everybody, take your cell phones and stay in touch!

Joe: You got it, Jack.

(music begins)

Cecelia: *(dreamily)* They probably have great mineral baths, and banquets…and they probably have closets full of fabulous dresses and wonderful robes, and jewels and everything. Oh, I don't have a thing to wear!

In a Palace

Words and Music by
PETER and HANNEKE JACOBS
Arranged by Peter Jacobs

24

News Crew

do my nails and hair. And an -

oth - er, to fan her face with air.

Choir In a pal - ace you'll find lux - u -

ries of ev - 'ry kind. You'll be wait - ed on and

28

one a nerv - ous wreck!

(Change scenery to the palace)

34

(During the instrumental interlude "In A Palace", the "mall" is transformed into the throne room inside of King Herod's Palace. This takes place in full view of the audience, as the song continues to the end.)

Levi: Introducing His Royal Highness, King Herod!

King Herod's Fanfare

PETER JACOBS

Choir in Unison: Long live King Herod! Long live King Herod! Long live King Herod!

Herod: *(entering from the side, parade waves at his subjects, the choir)* Ah, my loyal subjects! You may sit.

(The choir sits down on the risers. The News Crew, complete with all their camera gear, their crew bags and Cecelia's very large suitcase on wheels, begins to walk down the center aisle quarreling all the way. In the meantime, the Cherub Choir takes their place on the stage, either on risers next to the existing choir, or on the floor in front of the choir.)

Teri: Forget it Cece, I'm NOT carrying your bags for you. You practically have an entire cosmetic store in there.

Cece: Oh please, Teri!!! YOU don't have to go on the air! I mean, we're going to a PALACE… hello? You don't just show up at a palace looking like…well, like you!

(Levi, who is not supposed to allow anyone in the throne room unannounced, comes running out in front of the News Crew, bowing profusely before King Herod.)

Levi: Uh…Announcing the I Witness News reporters, Your Majesty.

Herod: *(confused and a bit perturbed)* The What?

Levi: The I Witness News reporters, Sire.

(The News Crew steps forward, Teri and Joe bow a bit awkwardly; Cecelia stands there.)

Joe: *(whispering loudly to Cecelia)* You have to bow, Cece!

Cece: Oh all right!

(she curtsies slightly)

Herod: *(with disdain)* And why have you come? Hmmmm?

Joe: *(stammering awkwardly)* Uh, well, Your Highness…we have heard that there are three Wise Men here and we would like to interview…

Herod: *(interrupting and shouting)* It is not my concern what you were told! I have no use for these peasants. Maybe they'd like a tour of the dungeon. *(Herod claps twice)* Guards! *(motions the guards to take them away)*

Cecelia: Hey, wait a minute, Mister! What do you think you're doing!!! Joe... *(the last part is muted as Joe put his hand over her mouth.)*

Levi: *(stage whispering to Herod)* Uh, Your Majesty, these are the ones I told you about… the ones who will make you famous!

Herod: Is this true? You will make me famous?

Teri: *(dryly)* In ways you can't even imagine, Your Highness.

Herod: *(immediately changing his tone)* So that all the kingdoms in the world will know my name?

Joe: Generations upon generations will know your name, Sire.

Herod: *(dismissing then with a wave)* Well, then I must go prepare myself for fame!…New robes, my hair must be just right…*(he gets up to leave)* See to it that these people are taken care of! *(mumbling to himself)* They're my friends.

Levi: *(again bowing low)* Yes, Your Majesty. *(Levi turns to the choir)* Long live King Herod!

Choir: *(echoing)* Long live King Herod! Long live King Herod! Long live King Herod!

(King Herod parade waves at the choir as he exits offstage)

Teri: *(sarcastically)* He's wound a bit tight, don't you think?

Levi: I apologize for His Highness. He's been a little bit grumpy lately…

Joe: Well, somebody should tell him that's no way to act…especially this time of year!

(music begins)

Nobody Likes a Grump at Christmas

Words and Music by
PETER and HANNEKE JACOBS
Arranged by Peter Jacobs

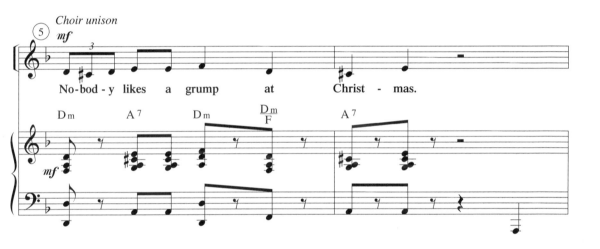

No-bod-y likes a frown, A smile turned up-side down That takes a-way my cheer. O!

No-bod-y likes a grump at Christ-mas.

No-bod-y likes a grump that's clear. While

40

CD: 20

(Cherub Choir quickly and quietly exit the stage. Director: Be sure to keep cherubs in their order when they sit back down, as they will reappear again later in the musical.)

Levi: *(apologetically to the News Crew)* Now, is there anything else I can get you to make you feel more comfortable?

Joe: No, we're fine, Levi. It's not necessary…

Cecelia: *(interrupting)* Well, I for one, would like a hot bath! And do you have some of those nice thick towels? What about a massage? Oh, and I could really use a pedicure…

Levi: Yes, ma'am. I will take you to your handmaiden now.

(Cecelia follows Levi out, after he picks up her suitcase and lugs it painstakingly offstage. Cecelia goes ahead of him, chattering as she leaves.)

Cecelia: *(as she leaves)* Levi, you've got a great place here…ya know, I've always thought that I should live in a palace…this is incredible…

(Teri and Joe begin to unpack their camera gear)

Teri: We've interviewed people much more famous than that old king! Just who does he think he is?

Simeon: *(approaching from the opposite side of the stage)* I would be careful what I said around here, Miss. These walls often have ears.

Joe: *(holding out his hand)* Oh, hello. I don't believe we've met? I'm Joe, and this is my associate, Teri.

Simeon: *(shaking Joe's hand)* My name is Simeon. I was summoned by His Majesty yesterday as soon as he heard about the star.

Teri: The Star? Oh, the UFO! So do you know something about it?

Simeon: *(looking around to make sure he's not being overheard)* Yes, I do. I have lived a long life, much of it filled with studying the Holy Scriptures. This star is mentioned in the Book of Numbers. It says, "There shall come a Star out of Jacob, and a King shall rise out of Israel."

Teri: A king?

Simeon: Not an ordinary king, mind you. This scripture refers to the star as a sign of the coming of the Messiah.

Joe: Hmm, I'll bet Herod has seen the star, too.

Simeon: I am sure that is why he summoned me, to find out what it meant. And when I told him about the Messiah, it sent him into a rage!

Teri: Yeah, another king would be competition for him!

Joe: So THAT'S why King Herod is so upset! He wants to get rid of that newborn king before he gets replaced!

Teri: And he's probably going to do anything he can to find this child and destroy Him.

Simeon: Yes, but God will never let that happen. I am an old man, now, but God has told me that before my life is over *(music begins)* I will indeed see this Messiah with my own eyes! And when I saw the star appear I knew that all my years of waiting would soon be over.

Could This Be the Messiah?

Words and Music by
PETER and HANNEKE JACOBS
Arranged by Peter Jacobs

50

new - born child_____ to come?_____

Ah,_____

F m⁷

D♭m⁶

35 *Simeon*

Could this be__ the Mes - si - ah, the One?_____

A♭/E♭

D♭m⁶/E♭

A♭2

CD: 25

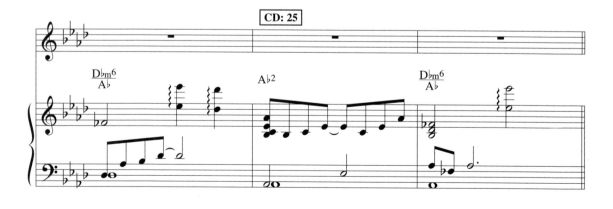

D♭m⁶/A♭

A♭2

D♭m⁶/A♭

52

54

(After the song, as the News Crew finishes setting up, King Herod is shown coming out from behind the choir. No one sees or hears him except the audience.)

Herod: *(scoffing)* Do they really think I don't listen to everything they say? Messiah indeed! There will be no Messiah as long as I live…*(turning to the choir)* and long may I live!

Choir: Long live King Herod! Long live King Herod!

Herod: *(not even looking at the choir)* Ahh…they love me!

(Herod sits down on his throne,. as Levi enters, hesitantly.)

Levi: Uh, Your Majesty?

Herod: What is it now, Levi?

Levi: Sire, you have more visitors!

Herod: Bring them to me at once!

Joe: Where is Cece?! We've got to film this! Teri, go find her. Quick!

Teri: I think I know JUST where to look!

(Teri runs out to find Cecelia)

Levi: Announcing the Three Wise Men from the East!

(music begins)

(The three Wise Men come down the aisle in a processional during the intro of the song. They arrive on stage in time to sing their solos.)

We Three Kings

Words and Music by
JOHN H. HOPKINS, JR.
Arranged by Peter Jacobs

*Play in absence of drum. If drum is used, continue rhythmic pattern through measure 38.

58

Guide us to thy per - fect light.

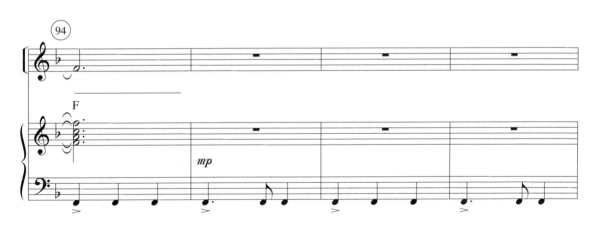

Guide us to thy per - fect light.

(After the song ends, the three Wise Men approach the throne and are quietly discussing things with Herod.)

Joe: *(pacing with his headphones on his ears)* Where is Cece? Oh, of all the times for her to wander off…

CD 33 SOUND EFFECTS: Cell Phone rings

Herod: What is that noise?

Joe: *(digging up his cell phone out of his bag)* Sorry, Your Majesty, Hello?

Jack: Hello? Joe, what's going on? Why aren't you guys on the air?

Joe: Teri's trying to find Cece, Jack! She's here somewhere!

Jack: Oh, for pity's sake! What is she up to now?!

(Teri comes out from the opposite side of the stage, dragging Cecelia along with her. Cecelia is in a bathrobe with a towel turbaned around her head.)

Cecelia: *(loudly protesting)* Teri! I was in the middle of getting my massage! And I'm in my bathrobe! I'm not coming out in public in my bathrobe with a towel on my head!

(The three Wise Men and Herod are wrapped up in their own conversation and oblivious to Cecelia.)

Teri: I found her, Joe! Not that she's gonna do us any good looking like this!

Joe: She's here, Jack. I gotta go! Bye *(click)*

Cecelia: Of all the lousy things to do, Teri, dragging me out of a perfectly good mineral bath! I was just starting to relax!

Joe: Relax!? Cece, the Three Wise Men are here! We have to go on the air RIGHT NOW!

Cecelia: Joe! Look at me! I can't go on the air like this!

Herod: *(suddenly addressing them threateningly)* What's going on over there? Are you quite ready to make me famous now? Because if you're NOT!!!

Joe: Uh, Yes, Your Majesty.

Teri: *(begins to count down)* In five, four, three, two…

Cecelia: *(during Teri's count-down)* What! Argh!!!

I Witness News Theme

PETER JACOBS

Copyright © 2000 by Pilot Point Music (ASCAP). All rights reserved.
Administered by The Copyright Company, 40 Music Square East, Nashville, TN 37203.

PLEASE NOTE: Copying of this product is NOT covered by CCLI licenses. For CCLI information call 1-800-234-2446.

Announcer: We take you now, live, via time-delay satellite, to Cecelia Barnhurst, reporting from Jerusalem. Cecelia?

(she looks mortified, then resolutely picks up the microphone)

Cecelia: Good afternoon. This is Cecelia Barnhurst, reporting from King Herod's Palace in Jerusalem. As you can clearly see *(embarrassed laugh)* I have been soaking in a royal mineral bath, which is among the finest in all the world. This stylish turban on my head is guaranteed to make one's hair soft as silk. Later on, I'll be showing you some of the fine cuisine served here at…

Joe: *(whispering fiercely)* CECE!! The Wise Men!!!

Cecelia: *(still smiling pseudo sweetly)* Oh yes. Here with His Majesty, King Herod, today are three Wise Men, who have come from the East to follow this unusual phenomenon in the skies over the greater Jerusalem metropolitan area…Yoo hoo, Mr. Wise Man, yes, just speak into the microphone here…could you please explain to our audience what that bright object is in the sky?

Wise Man 1: Yes. For several weeks now, this bright new star has appeared over my country and I felt compelled to follow it to see where it led.

Cecelia: And what about the rest of you? Did you all come from the same place?

Wise Man 2: Actually we met on the road. While our camels were drinking from the well, we discovered that we were all following the same star.

Wise Man 3: We believe that the star leads to the birthplace of a newborn king, one sent from heaven above. And we are all very anxious to see him.

Wise Man 1: I'm sure King Herod, here, feels the same way!

Cecelia: Is this true, Your Majesty?

(Herod, suddenly put on the spot. begins speaking like a politician)

Herod: Well, Ms. Barnhurst, I have long been a card carrying member of the Future Kings Association. And I can tell you today that I plan on giving this new king *(pseudo sweetly)* everything He has coming to Him.

Cecelia: So then, Your Majesty, will you also go to visit this newborn king?

Herod: *(laying it on thickly)* No, no, I believe it is my kingly duty to stay here and carry on my work for my loyal subjects. But I would like to invite my three guests here to stop on their way back, for a royal reception. Yes, I would very much like to know the whereabouts of this, uh, newborn king. That way I can find Him later…to pay my respects, of course.

Wise Man 1, 2, 3: As you wish, Your Highness. *(all bow to Herod)*

Cecelia: Thank you all for allowing us to be here on this momentous occasion. *(turning again to the camera)* And now, I believe it's about time for my appointment at the palace's hair salon! This is Cecelia Barnhurst reporting from King Herod's throne room in Jerusalem.

Teri: And we're clear…Nice save, Cece!

Cecelia: I can't believe you guys made me go on the air that way! I am SO EMBARRASED! Aurgh!

(she turns and stomps offstage)

Wise Man 1: *(bowing to King Herod)* Your Highness, we must take our leave now. The star is coming out again soon and we must follow it so that we may find this newborn king.

Herod: *(dismissing them with a wave)* Yes, yes, yes, whatever. Have a pleasant journey.

(three Wise Men exit offstage)

Herod: So, when will you people do MY interview??!!

Joe: *(confused)* Uh, excuse me, Your Majesty?

Herod: MY interview! The one where you make ME famous?! Because if you're NOT…

Joe: *(interrupting him nervously)* Uh, well I'm sure we can fit that in tomorrow morning, Your Highness.

Herod: It better be tomorrow!. You are dismissed.

(Joe, Teri and Levi all bow and exit offstage, leaving their bags behind)

Herod: *(beginning to fantasize about fame)* Tomorrow…Oh yes, tomorrow I will become famous. Tomorrow the entire world will see this handsome face.

(music begins)

Herod's Song

Words and Music by
PETER and HANNEKE JACOBS
Arranged by Peter Jacobs

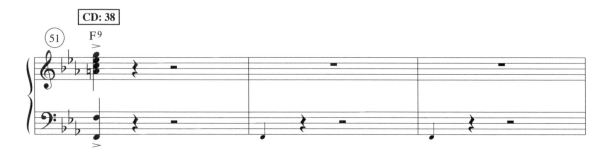

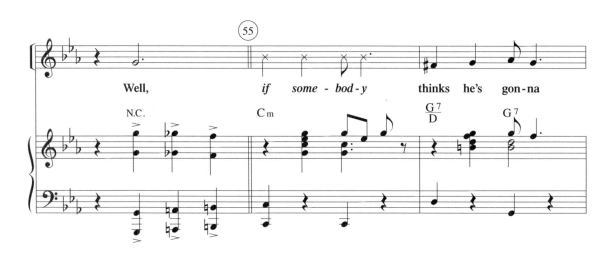

Well, *if some - bod - y* thinks he's gon - na

take this crown a - way,_____ *For - feit - ing his*

HEROD: Ah, Sing it with me! (71)

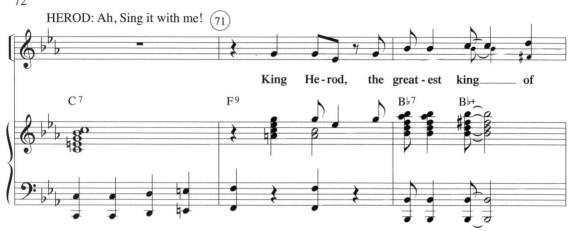

King He-rod, the great-est king_____ of

HEROD: That's me! *(laughs)*

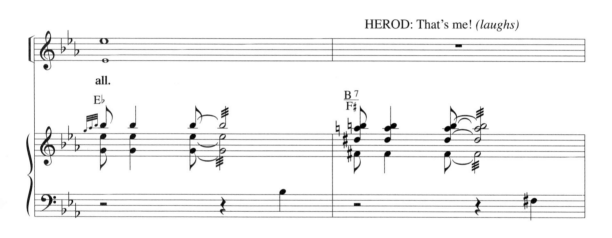

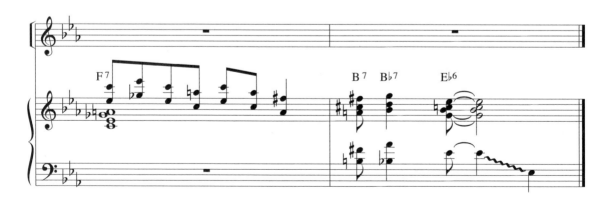

Herod: *(at end of song)* I must go! I have lots to do!

(Immediately after the song, Herod lifts up his robe and begins to exit offstage. He trips over Joe's bag, and kicks it angrily.)

Herod: Levi, those News Crew people left their bags! Get someone to clean this up.
    (suddenly a thought occurs to him) Wait, just a moment. What have we here…
    hmmmm.

(Herod reaches in to retrieve two cell phones out of the bag and hides it in his robe. Immediately, he exists offstage. Simeon, Joe, Cecelia and Teri peek around the corner, nervously coming back onstage and looking around to see if King Herod is still around.)

Teri: Joe! Is the coast clear?

Joe: *(looking around and behind things to make sure Herod isn't hiding somewhere)* I think
    so…Yep, he's gone!

Simeon: His majesty has a bit of a temper, I'm afraid…

Teri: Ya think?

Joe: Well, we're leaving anyway, so it doesn't matter. Simeon, what's the fastest way to
    Bethlehem? I'd like to get there before the three Wise Men do.

Simeon: Well, most people travel by camel, but…

Cecelia: *(interrupting)* Ugh! Those smelly beasts? You couldn't pay me to get on one of those
    awful things!

Simeon: Well, I don't think you'll need to worry about that, my dear. All the camels in the
    entire city were rented out long ago. Caesar has required everyone to go back to the
    city of their birth, to pay their tax.

Cecelia: *(sigh)* Fine. So we'll take a chariot. Surely there must be a spare chariot in a palace!

Simeon: I'm afraid the chariots are only for the King's use, ma'am.

Cecelia: *(without thinking)* Okay, I'll go ask him.

Joe: *(stopping her)* Cece, think about it. You're going to ask Herod if we can borrow a chariot, so we can leave, before we do his interview tomorrow?

Cecelia: *(realizing her mistake)* Right, got it.

Teri: *(slinging her camera bag over her shoulder)* Well, I guess it looks like we're gonna have to walk then!

Cecelia: Excuuuuuse me, but there is NO WAY I'm going to walk all the way to Bethlehem! Besides, I haven't finished my facial.

Joe: We don't have time for that, Cece! The three Wise Men are leaving RIGHT NOW, and we have to follow them or we won't make it to Bethlehem in time.

Cecelia: Do you know what traveling in the desert will do to my face and my hair?

Simeon: *(to Cecelia)* Well, I know a journey through the desert is not what you had planned, but it seems clear to me that all of you were sent here to witness a much greater plan.

Teri: What do you mean? What plan?

Simeon: The prophet, Isaiah, put it like this: "As the heavens are higher than the earth, so are My ways higher than your ways…" *(Isaiah 55:8,9)* I know, try thinking about it like this…

(music begins)

Perfect for You

Words and Music by
PETER and HANNEKE JACOBS
Arranged by Peter Jacobs

78

(to pg. 76, meas. 13)

82

Cecelia: Well, plan or no plan, I'm not wearing a bathrobe to travel in! I'll be right back! *(exits quickly)*

Joe: *(calling after her)* You've got 5 minutes, Cece!

Simeon: May God bless your journey! I'll be praying for you the entire time! Godspeed and goodbye!

News Crew: Bye, Simeon!

Simeon: Good bye.

(Simeon and the rest of the News Crew exit offstage. On the opposite side of the stage, King Herod reappears.)

Herod: *(shouting)* Levi!! Levi!!

(Levi comes running in and bows down before him)

Levi: *(quivering)* You summoned me, Your Majesty?

Herod: *(proudly holding up two cell phones)* Look what I found, Levi!

Levi: What ARE those things, Your Majesty?

Herod: Magical communication devices, Levi! They allow you to talk to someone else who is far away! I took them right out of those people's bags! *(snickering)*

Levi: Uh, what are you going to do with them, Sire?

Herod: You will take ONE of these devices with you, and I will keep the other here.

Levi: And Sire, where am I supposed to go?

Herod: Follow those reporters, Levi! They will take you straight to this, to this so-called king! Then, when you have found him, you will tell me EXACTLY where he is! I will send my soldiers, and this future king will be no more! *(laughs)* Brilliant idea, if I do say so myself!

Levi: *(echoing)* Brilliant, Your Majesty.

Herod: Now GO, Levi! Don't lose sight of them! And after you have told me where this
     newborn child is, bring these reporters back! I can still use them to make me famous!

Levi: As you wish, Your Highness. *(Levi runs offstage)*

Herod: NO ONE WILL EVER TAKE MY PLACE! NO ONE!

(he laughs wickedly and follows Levi offstage)

Scene Change Underscore

PETER JACOBS

*(King Herod's throne is quickly removed while a pup tent and a fake fire are quickly put up.
Three shepherds are seen roasting marshmallows over the fire. The News Crew begins to drag
their way down the aisle with suitcases on wheels and their camera gear in tow.)*

Cecelia: *(whining)* Oh, my feet hurt!

Teri: Yeah, I know. I'm pretty tired, too.

Joe: Look, there's some shepherds up ahead. Let's just camp out with them tonight. We all
     need a break.

Cecelia: Camp out with shepherds? Oh, please! I'd rather go find a rock to sleep on by myself!!!

CD 48 SOUND EFFECTS: Baying Wolves
(The New Crew stops dead in their tracks.)

Cecelia: On second thought…

(they walk over to the shepherds)

Joe: Hi guys, what's up?

Shepherd 1: Aww, nothin'. We're just sittin' here, watchin' the sheep, havin' some marshmallows. Care for one?

Cecelia: Uh, none for me…thanks. I just need to get off my feet!

Joe: Well, I'm gonna unpack my camera. I gotta get a shot of that star!

(He puts his jacket on, then get the camera out and looks through the lens up at the star.)

Shepherd 2: It's a beautiful night tonight, we're going to sleep outside. If you ladies want to sleep in a tent, make yourself at home.

Cecelia: *(to herself)* I could have been soaking in a nice, hot mineral bath right about now.

Shepherd 1: We'd all better get some sleep.

Shepherd 2: Yeah, the sun comes up real early.

(everyone says good night and lies down on blankets)

(music begins)

(The News Crew and the Shepherds wake up startled! One person dressed as the Angel of the Lord stands before them. Option: the Angel of the Lord can say his or her own lines if desired…or he or she can pantomime as the Announcer narrates the passage from Luke 2 :9-14.)

Angels Underscore
with
Hark! the Herald Angels Sing

PETER JACOBS
Arranged by Peter Jacobs

*Narration begins

*NARRATION: And behold an angel of the Lord stood before them, and the glory of the Lord shone round about them; and they were greatly afraid.

Then the angel said to them, "Fear not: for, behold, I bring you good tidings of great joy, which will be to all people. For unto you is born this day in the city of David a Savior, which is Christ the Lord. And this shall be a sign unto you; You will find the babe wrapped in swaddling clothes, lying in a manger."

And suddenly there was with the angel a multitude of the heavenly hosts praising God, and saying, "Glory to God in the highest, and on earth peace, good will towards men." *(Luke 2:9-14)*

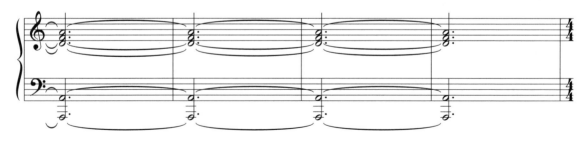

*"Hark! the Herald Angels Sing"

Segue to "Angels We Have Heard on High"

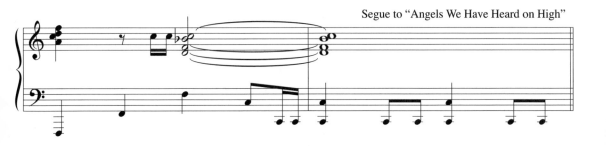

Angels We Have Heard on High

Traditional French Carol
Arranged by Peter Jacobs

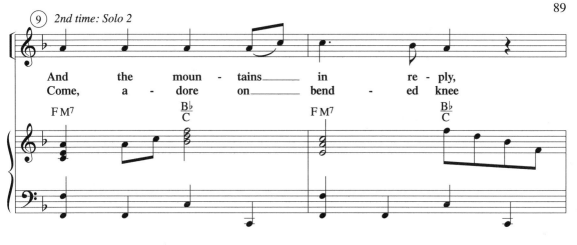

(9) *2nd time: Solo 2*

And   the   moun - tains_____ in   re - ply,
Come,   a - dore   on_____ bend - ed knee

F M⁷ B♭/C F M⁷ B♭/C

CD: 51 1st time
CD: 53 2nd time

Ech - o - ing   their_____ joy - ous strains.
Christ,   the   Lord,   our_____ new - born King.

F M⁷ B♭/C C¹³ F

(13) *Both times: descant*

Glo - - - -

Both times: Choir

Glo - - - -

(13) F D Gm C

Shepherds and News Crew: *(ad lib)* Wow! That was unbelievable! etc.

Shepherd 2: We MUST go see this newborn baby who was born tonight in Bethlehem!
        Come on! *(the shepherds hurry offstage)*

Joe: Never in my wildest dreams…

Cecelia: *(in awe)* Those were real angels, Joe! I mean, real live…

CD 54 SOUND EFFECTS: Cell phone rings

(She is interrupted by a cell phone ringing nearby. Seen by the audience, Levi is behind a rock and frantically pushing buttons on the phone to get it to stop ringing.)

Joe: What's that?

Teri: Your cell phone's ringing in your backpack, Joe. It's probably Jack.

Joe: That's not coming from my backpack! It's coming from behind that rock!…
        (cell phone continues ringing)

Levi: *(puzzledly looking into the phone)* Hello?

Jack: *(in the newsroom area)* Hello? Who IS this?

(by this time, Joe finds him and drags him out from behind a rock)

Joe, Cecelia and Teri: LEVI!

Teri: What are you doing with Joe's phone?

Jack: Well, whoever you are, Levi, let me speak to Joe!

(obediently, Levi hands the phone to Joe)

Joe: Jack, it's me now.

Jack: What on earth is going on over there, Joe? And who is this Levi fellow?

Joe: It would take too long to explain, Jack.

Jack: Well, you left your camera on, and it recorded something strange! I can't believe I'm really asking this, but, Joe…were those ALIENS?!

Joe: It happened while we were asleep, Jack. I didn't even know I was filming! But Jack, those were angels! Real angels, Jack! Jack? Hello?!

Joe: Arghh! We must've lost the connection.

Cecelia: *(accusingly to Levi)* Well, I for one, would like to know why you've been following us, Levi!?

Teri: Yeah, and what were you doing with Joe's cell phone!?

Levi: *(stammering)* His majesty, King Herod, sent me to spy on you. And I'm sorry, I really am! Oh, please spare my life!

Cecelia: *(angrily)* King Herod sent you to spy on US?

Joe: What about my cell phone? How did you get that?

Levi: *(miserably)* His Majesty took two of your magical devices. He wanted me to follow you. And when you found the newborn king, I was to use the device to tell him where he could send soldiers to destroy the baby.

Joe: I THOUGHT that was his plan!

Teri: But we didn't think he'd use US to carry it out!!!

Levi: *(miserably)* Oh, please, I ask you again, please spare my life.

Joe: We're not going to hurt you, Levi.

Levi: But I thought…after seeing those angels singing from heaven to you…and those magical devices…

Teri: Believe me, Levi, cell phones aren't magic. And we've never seen angels before either.

Levi: What are you going to do with me, then?

Joe: Well, *(thinking)* I guess we're just gonna have to take you with us.

Cecelia: *(excitedly)* Well, what are we waiting for! Let's go!

Teri: *(surprised)* Hello? Cece? Are you feeling all right? I thought your feet hurt. Joe, did she just say what I thought I heard her say?

Cecelia: *(resolutely)* Teri, some things are more important than sore feet! If God went to all that trouble to send angels to tell us about this child being born, we've got to get over there so we can film Him. The whole world needs to know that the Messiah is born!

Joe: *(suddenly seeing the whole picture)* Cece, you're right! That's what God's plan is all about! We have to tell the world!

(News Crew exits quickly offstage with their gear)

(music begins)

(During the next song, the shepherds' tent and campfire are quickly removed and replaced with the nativity scene. Joseph and Mary, carrying Baby Jesus enter from stage left and take their places center stage.)

Go, Tell It on the Mountain

JOHN W. WORK, JR.

Afro-American Spiritual
Arranged by Peter Jacobs

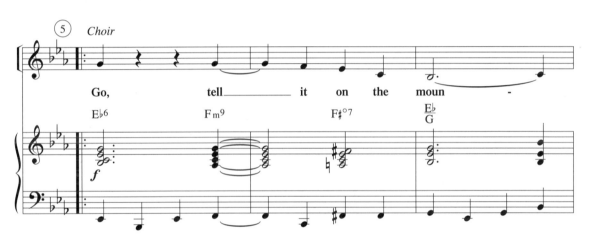

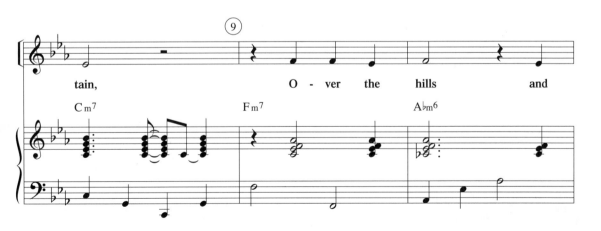

96

102

(The News Crew re-enters the stage from stage right, and quickly begin to set up their equipment. Levi looks uncomfortable and stays fairly hidden in a corner.)

Joe: *(over his shoulder as he is setting up)* Levi, don't you want to come in and see the Messiah?

Levi: Uh…I just don't want to be in your pictures, Joe.

Joe: Why not?

Levi: *(miserably)* I'm afraid that His Majesty, King Herod, will find out that I have betrayed him. And then, off goes my head.

Joe: But Levi, are you ever really going back to that palace?

Levi: Where else would I go? It's the only place I know.

Joe: Surely you can make another life for yourself outside of the palace, Levi. But this day your Messiah is born! Levi, come in and SEE Him!

Teri: Stand by, everybody. In 5, 4, 3, 2, *(she motions for "1" and points to Cecelia)*

(music begins)

(Option: Cherub Choir takes their place next to or on front of the regular choir.)

Cecelia: *(excitedly)* Good morning to each and every man, woman and child! We come to you on this Christmas morning from the small town of Bethlehem in Judea, where we are extremely privileged to be witnessing the arrival of a long-awaited child, just born to Mary and Joseph. This child will become the Savior of the world, the Christ child himself, the Messiah! Many have journeyed long and far to see this miracle of God. Let's watch as these events unfold before our eyes.

(Both choirs sing and invite the audience to participate. During the song, the shepherds come down the aisle and kneel before the Baby in the manger. Then Teri and Cecelia come from onstage and they also kneel before the Baby. Joe kneels as he films. Then, lastly, the three Wise Men come down the aisle, bring their gifts and kneel.)

O Come, All Ye Faithful

Words and Music by
JOHN F. WADE and
PETER and HANNEKE JACOBS
Arranged by Peter Jacobs

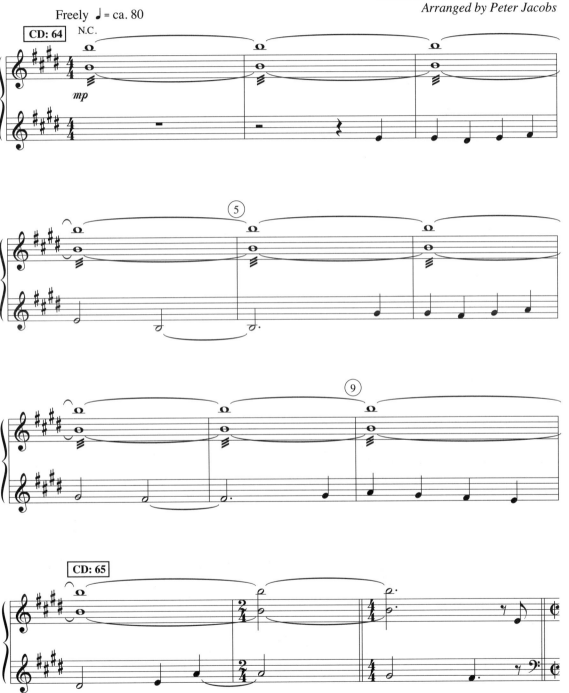

Divisi

Choir 1

Come and be - hold Him

Choir 2

Come and be - hold Him

G♯m   C♯+   C♯   F♯m   C♯/E♯

born the King of an - gels! O

born the King of an - gels!

F♯/A♯   E/G♯   F♯/A♯   B   B7   B sus

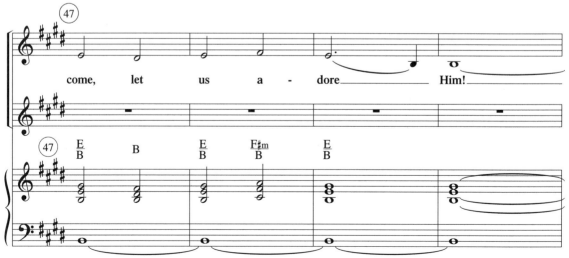

come, let us a - dore_____ Him!_____

E/B   B   E/B   F♯m/B   E/B

112

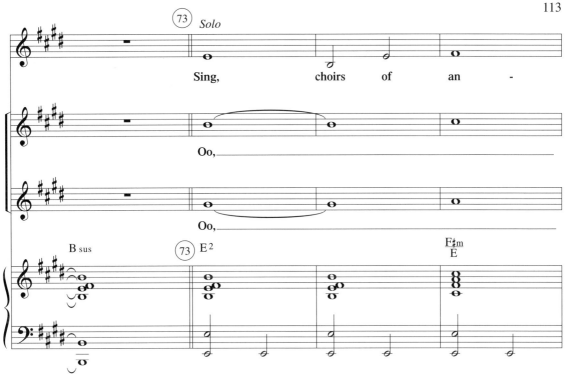

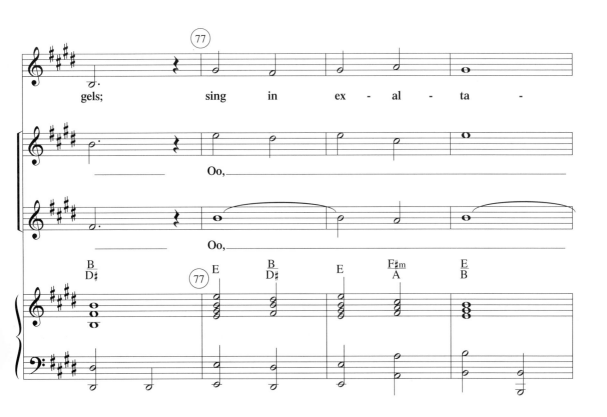

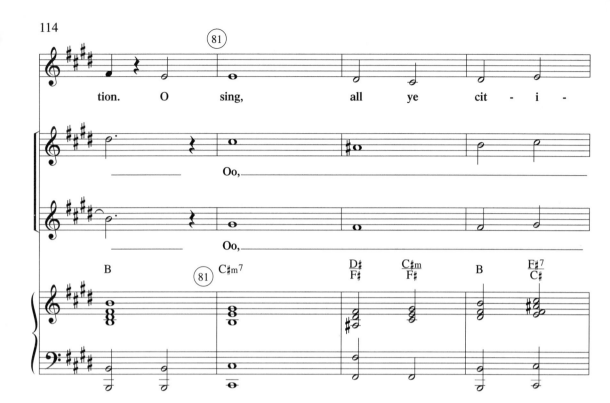

tion.　O　sing,　　all　ye　cit – i –

Oo,

Oo,

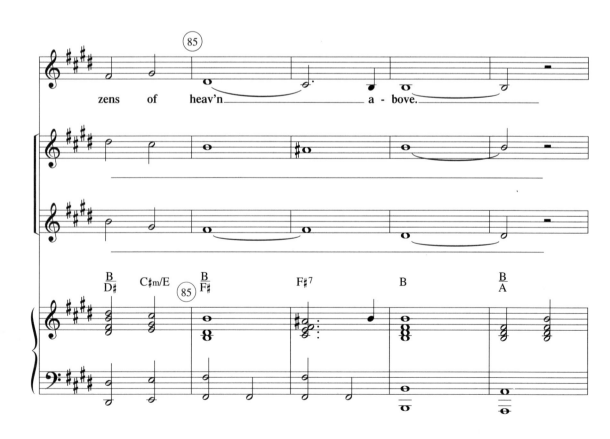

zens　of　heav'n　　　　　a – bove.

116

118

Joe: Teri, take the camera for a second.

(Teri takes the camera while Joe goes up to a still hesitating Levi)

(music begins "Levi's Prayer")

Joe: Levi, Simeon taught us a scripture from Isaiah, just before we left the palace. It goes like this, "…As the heavens are higher than the earth, so are My ways higher than your ways." You see, Levi, God has a plan…even for you.

Levi: God has a plan? Even for me? What more can I ask for?

(Levi then approaches, timidly, but resolutely and kneels down in full sight of Joe's camera.)

Levi: *(praying)* Dear Lord, today I take my life and give it to You. You are my newborn Messiah and my King. All that I have and all that I am, is now forever Yours.

Joe: *(quietly)* Good for you, Levi.

Levi: *(suddenly bold)* Today is the day we have all been waiting for! A miracle has arrived! Today God gave us our Messiah!

Cecelia: *(still on camera)* And on this special day, we have also come to realize that God has a plan, a plan for each of us. If we choose to follow this plan, then we will have the assurance that we can trust God to take care of us, wherever He may take us. *(music ends)* May we never forget what we have seen on this very special Christmas! This is Cecelia Barnhurst, for I Witness News.

(music begins)

Levi's Prayer

Underscore

JOHN F. WADE and
PETER JACOBS
Arranged by Peter Jacobs

Hear the Bells of Christmas

Words and Music by
PETER and HANNEKE JACOBS
Arranged by Peter Jacobs

124

heav'n a-bove, Their bless-ed tid-ings bring.

*"I Heard the Bells on Christmas Day"

Hear the bells of Christ-mas ring through-out the

(This is a "False Ending". The audience will think the musical is over at this point. The cast and choir should hold their poses at the end until the applause completely dies down. Then, suddenly...)

CD 79 SOUND EFFECTS: Cell Phone rings

Joe: Jack? Did you see that? Wait, who IS this? King Herod?!! You want to talk to Levi? Let me see if he's here...*(covering up the mouthpiece of the phone)* What do you want to do, Levi?

Levi: *(to Joe)* Now that I have seen my Messiah, I am not afraid to die. If the King wants to send soldiers to destroy me, I am ready to go.

Joe: *(into the cell phone)* Uh, Your Majesty? Levi can't come to the phone right now. What's that? Calm down, Sire. *(Joe listens for a while)* Uh, huh. Hmm. Uh, huh...You know, I'm having trouble hearing you, Sire. These cell phones don't always work the way they should. But I know how you can fix that. Just go ahead and take your phone right over to your mineral bath. Yes, that's right and when I tell you hold it over the water and just drop it in. Yeah, it should work fine in a few minutes, sir. Ready? Drop it. Hello? *(he winks at Levi)*

(he hangs up his own cell phone as everyone cheers)

(music begins)

Go, Tell It on the Mountain
Reprise

JOHN W. WORK, JR.

Afro-American Spiritual
Arranged by Peter Jacobs

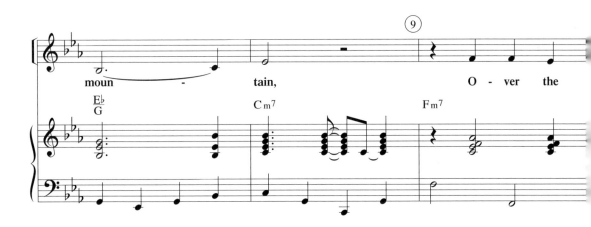

STAGING DIRECTIONS

The staging needs for this musical are minimal, mostly consisting of a few props brought in to set each scene. The news room set remains in place in the background, while the other "sets" are moved quickly in and out.

News Room Set

A small table is set up behind Jack. On top of the table is a computer, a fax machine, and a cell phone. Optional background props might include an ON AIR sign, etc. This setup should be put into a corner of the stage and should stay set up.

Mall Set

The mall set only appears in the beginning of the musical and is set up at the very beginning. We recommend portable signs which can be quickly and easily removed. If there is no background set on which to hang these signs, just attach them to long sticks and put them into a bucket with florist clay, and fill with moss or greenery.

King Herod's Throne Room

A large, preferably gilded throne is visible (possibly elevated on a large box to give it a larger-than-life quality.) Be careful, however, as the throne will need to be moved in and out quickly.

Shepherd's Camp

A small pup tent and a "portable" fire pit. We recommend making the fire pit in a large, round sledding coaster, cover with foil and insert "flames" made from cellophane wrap. Several small flashlights hidden in the folds of the wrap will provide the "flame." (Don't forget the coat hanger-fashioned marshmallow roasters!)

Nativity Scene

Any staging for this is optional, since the grouping of the Biblical characters is clearly understood. However, if you wish to bring in a manger filled with hay, the "Baby Jesus" can be placed in it.

Don't worry about staging the miracle of the angels singing to the shepherds. This event is watched by the actors on the stage, as if it is taking place in the audience. The music will help accomplish this, and both the reporters and the shepherds should "react" and point to the "angels" as if they are seeing them in one designated spot in the audience.

I WITNESS NEWS: LIVE FROM BETHLEHEM